The Glove Box Guide

Every Driver and Auto-Owner's
Indispensable Guide to Preserving Your
Investment and Maximizing Safety

A Pudge-Endorsed Guide

LAUREN BRAUSEN

CONTENTS

ACKNOWLEDGEMENTS

Pudge. This book would not exist if not for him. A grease monkey from the very beginning, my brother, Steve (aka Pudge), has guided me in all things automotive.

His relentless patience as he coached his sister in getting her two feet to work the three pedals (gas, brake and clutch) on that old 1960 manual transmission panel truck was above and beyond the call of duty. He had me poised at a stop sign at the top of the hill on the steepest road around.

Somehow my little brother knew he could talk me through cresting the incline and ultimately making it into and through that daunting intersection. He knew I could hold that baby in gear, left foot warily letting the clutch out without totally jerking the transmission out its mounts, lickety-split get my right foot off the brake and onto the gas, and get 'er moving forward without rolling too horribly far backwards down the hill. His belief in my ability moved mountains for me.

Consistent with the self-mastery life paths of my other two brothers, it's no surprise that Pudge grew up to be a master auto mechanic... and my ultimate fact-checker for this publication.

When my own children learned to drive in the late 1990's (by then most everyone was driving automatic transmissions), there was no question but that they would learn on a manual transmission. Granted, that Honda Accord could not begin to rival the driving experience of that old "Pudgemobile", but I still couldn't have been prouder knowing that my kids had mastered, what many consider challenging, the manual transmission.

Jacques from Norm's Tires, and also father of my children, similarly holds a place for my gratitude. He fielded many a question that he, no doubt, rolled his eyes at while wondering how I came up with such trifling questions. But those little details were necessary to putting together the right words to explain and clarify a point to a potentially novice reader.

My deepest thanks to Pudge, Jacques, Dan and David for everything, big and small, you have ever done for me.

INTRODUCTION

An outright must-read for new and younger drivers, even most veteran drivers will discover surprising and seriously helpful car care tips in The Glove Box Guide. Your vehicle's owner's manual contains a wealth of useful information, but reading it is tedious and long. Crammed with valuable insights in a quick, easy-to-read format, this guidebook is intended to complement your owner's manual with quick descriptions and simple instructions designed to "save the day" when dealing with car ownership challenges.

Kept short to provide important fundamental car care information and valuable tips without bogging down the reader, remember that the brevity is for your convenience, but brief does not mean unimportant.

We urge you to consider each point in this guidebook seriously to help you **stay safe on the road** AND **preserve your financial investment**.

vii

CHAPTER 1

CARS

Second only to a home, your car is probably your most expensive possession, and your unrivaled means of mobility and independence. Where would YOU be without your automobile? For most people, the answer to that question is "Lost."

Automobile-dependent, we take our cars for granted, overlooking the fact that we take our life and the lives of those around us into our hands every single time we get behind the wheel. We literally entrust our safety to each and every car we pass on the road, blindly expecting that they are and will continue being safe roadway companions. It is every driver's personal and societal responsibility to maintain a safe vehicle and to be a conscientious motorist. And a well-earned bonus for doing that is financial gain.

This guide is the perfect resource to help you:

- Maximize the longevity of your vitally essential automobile

- Spend your automotive dollars wisely
- Prevent time-consuming, schedule-disruptive automotive troubles
- Avoid accidents from fender-benders to crippling crashes - or worse
- Enjoy a more comfortable ride

Before getting into the nitty gritty of car care, here are some totally free ways to prevent repair bills and even save lives:

- **Driving requires your attention.** Texting or accessing the internet on a wireless device while driving is a bad idea and a bad habit. Don't do it.

- **Do not drink and drive**. Do you really want to increase your likelihood of committing manslaughter? And even if the hospitalized victim (which could be you) doesn't die, do you want that to be the life you wake up to the next morning? Even if there is no resulting accident, if you get caught driving over the legal limit, you can land yourself in a legal and financial nightmare.

- **Stay aware** of the fact that the other guy may not be paying attention. I can't stress this enough. Especially these days when we are wont to be distracted by while driving. Modern technology has created an unstable driving environment.

While we cannot control whether or not the other guy is being attentive, we can control our own attentiveness. And we can bear in mind that he may not be paying attention. On a second's notice, we may have to react to and adjust for that other guy's error.

See the Governors Highway Safety Association website www.ghsa.org for a lot of useful driving information and for U.S. state-specific cell phone and texting laws.

- **Tailgating** is the cause of most rear-end collisions. **Maintain enough distance** between you and the guy in front of you. Make sure that if he stops short, you'll have sufficient space to stop before you slam into his back end. Hit the backside of the car in front of you and it's your fault. It's **your** responsibility to leave enough space between you and him (one car length for every 10 mph you are moving). Do not tailgate. Por favor.

- **Avoid driving behind vehicles** that are **hauling things**: A trunk bungeed closed, the bed of a pickup truck filled with odds and ends, a mattress strapped to a roof, a trailer loaded with firewood or scrap. Do not assume people have objects properly secured during transit. Many do not. Be prepared for things to come loose and bounce wild and far across the asphalt. Your best bet is to get the heck away from them as quickly as possible. Change lanes, speed up to get past them, slow down to create **a lot of** sufficient space – just don't drive right behind them.

- **Road rage** has never benefitted anyone in any way. So the other guy did

something you thought was stupid?
Who hasn't? On or off the road, we all
do stupid things sometimes. We are just
a bunch of humans all trying to get
where we each are going. If someone
cuts you off, defer the space to them
and let them go. If someone is rudely
driving right on your tail, try to get out of
their way and let them pass. In five
minutes the incident is going to be
completely meaningless. Let it go.
If you haven't cut anyone else off yet,
you will. Sometimes drivers cut other
drivers off with intention and sometimes
it's unintentional. But in no case is it
worth it turning it into road rage. If for no
other reason, drop it for your own
health. Let's all play nice and work
together making traveling a pleasant
and efficient experience. Besides, you
never know when the other guy might
be packing a .357 and perfectly willing
to use it. Let the rage go. Play nice. Be
kind. Cultivate peace.
In these situations, I like to actually
verbalize a kind comment. They can't
hear me, of course, but, for example, I'll
lighten up on the gas pedal and allow
space for the encroaching driver and

say, "Here you go fellow citizen of the planet, here's some extra space for you to enter." This not only keeps things smoother on the road, it keeps my stress level down... and can even be downright self-entertaining.

- **Defer to truckers.** Their vehicles are demanding, their responsibilities huge, their schedules usually tight, and our roadways are their workplace. If you are in their path and going slower than them, get over. And do not assume truckers can see you. Well really, don't assume any other driver sees you, but especially truckers. Big rigs have a different visual capacity than cars. If there is something you can do to make their trek easier, do it. Moving stuff around the surface of the planet is what we humans mostly do, and truckers play a huge role in that. Like trash collectors and military personnel, truckers deserve a special thank you.

- As well as anything else lying in the road, **avoid running over bungee cords**. The hooks on the ends of them can take your tire out. It's not uncommon to see bungee cords in the road. Why is that? Well, remember those loaded vehicles we want avoid driving behind because their load may not be properly secured? Yup, bungee cord fell off. Hope no one was driving too close behind them when that happened.

- The majority of cars on the road have electric **fuel pumps** inside the gas tank. The gas in the tank is a coolant for the fuel pump. A gas tank below ¼ full no longer keeps the pump fully submerged, making the pump susceptible to overheating. Many mechanics agree this temperature increase can cause fuel pump failure. Besides eliminating the possibility of running out of gas, keeping your tank over ¼ full might also prevent having to replace your fuel pump.

- Slow down when driving through **parking lots.** There are cars pulling in, cars pulling out and pedestrians coming and going. Practice extra patience and courtesy in parking lots.

At the end of this book there's a "Maintenance Log" for recording services you have performed, including the mileage and date. It'll help keep you on track with getting services scheduled on time, plus logged information is a selling point at time of resale.

You might be amazed at the priceless safety and monetary rewards you reap by taking proper car of your auto. Google him and you'll find Mr. Irv Gordon who has driven his 1966 Volvo P1800 over 3 **million miles!** It's still in great shape and going strong simply because he's taken great care of it.

CHAPTER 2

MOTOR OIL

Routinely changing the oil and oil filter in your car is the single-most important thing you can do for your car. Got it? **The single-most important thing!** Motor oil has the highly critical job of lubricating the engine's moving parts, reducing friction, buffering heat, and keeping the engine clean. Well-maintained oil:

- Prevents engine breakdown
- Improves engine performance
- Adds tens of thousands of miles (or more) to the life of your engine

As oil circulates through your engine, it carries away destructive debris generated from the heat, metals, and dirt in the engine. As the oil passes through the oil filter, the filter hangs onto the contaminated particles. The filter can't sift out every contaminant, but even if it could, a filter can only hold so much waste. If you don't change the filter at appropriate intervals, deadly debris continually circulates through your engine, wreaking havoc.

Oil degrades over time, losing its lubricant properties. Degraded oil makes it increasingly harder for engine parts to move, and metal starts grinding against metal. This added stress creates even more harmful waste product, which can quickly and severely damage your entire engine.

If enough parts break down, they can jam up or fuse together - a death knell to your engine. Your engine could stop working or even explode. It's important to change the oil before contamination levels reach a point where engine damage can occur. **Degraded or dirty oil cannot do its job. It must be changed to prevent damage to your engine.** If you think oil changes are expensive or inconvenient, how much time and money do you suppose replacing the whole engine will set you back?

Some mechanics recommend changing petroleum-based motor oil, and the filter, every 2,000 to 3,000 miles, others say 3,500 to 7,500 miles. Some higher-end oils can get by with changing just the filter (and not the oil) for some intervals, but even those oils need to be changed when their time is up. Consult your owner's manual or mechanic about what type and weight oil is best for your car and driving conditions.

<u>SYNTHETIC OIL</u>

Synthetic oil provides superior engine lubrication, which can improve engine operation, resulting in longer engine life and better fuel efficiency. Synthetic oil costs more than petroleum-based oil, but the cost can be offset by its longer lifespan.

Synthetic motor oil offers advantages over traditional petroleum-based oil. Synthetic oil:

- Is free of destructive impurities found in petroleum-based oil
- Performs better and more consistently at higher engine temperatures
- Is likely to fall in price as production methods improve (traditional oil prices will likely rise along with the price of crude oil)
- Needs to be changed less often, creating less need for disposal of waste oil

Petroleum-based motor oil thickens in colder temperatures, forcing the starter and battery to work harder to start a cold engine. Synthetic oil is not as affected by cold so it flows easier at start-up. Synthetic motor oil is more likely right for you if you:

- Drive in very hot or very cold weather
- Tow heavy loads

Check your owner's manual or ask your service advisor if synthetic motor oil may be right for your vehicle.

HOW TO CHECK MOTOR OIL

1) Turn off the engine and open the hood.

2) Locate the oil dipstick. If you aren't sure where it is, check your owner's manual or ask your mechanic.

3) Pull out the dipstick and wipe it clean with a rag. (Note where you pull the dipstick from.)

4) Put the dipstick back into the hole and push it back in *all the way*.

Dipstick wiped clean

5) Remove the dipstick again and see where the oil residue is in relation to

Dipstick with oil

the indicators marked on the stick. In this image, there is an "F" indicating the "full" level. Dipsticks may vary slightly in appearance.

If the oil level on the dipstick is low, add oil. (The oil on the dipstick in the photo is clean oil. Your oil will likely be darker.)

HOW TO ADD MOTOR OIL

1) Add oil through the oil-filler hole located at the top of the engine. Add ¼ qt. (250 ml) at a time to avoid overfilling. Use a funnel to

avoid spills.

2) Recheck the oil level, following steps 3 through 6 from "How to check oil" above until the dipstick indicates the proper amount of oil.

CHAPTER 3

TIRES

This is where the rubber meets the road. **Your tires are the *number one safety component* on your vehicle!**

The part of your car with the greatest safety responsibility is your tires, and the correct amount of air pressure in them is **VITAL** for tires to function properly and safely.

Too much or too little air pressure:

- Impairs critically necessary traction, braking, and steering abilities
- Predisposes your tires to failure
- Reduces gas mileage

Tires do not "blow out" for no reason. Improper inflation is the most common reason tires blow out.

Tires heat up during driving. As tire air pressure decreases, the temperature of the tire rubber (while in motion) increases. A tire running with low air pressure will run hotter and hotter, setting the stage for a blowout. Air-pressure-related failure can happen very quickly and can be deadly.

If you feel a tire right after driving and it's too hot to hold your hand on, the air pressure is too low and you're on your way to a blowout. **Get air promptly.** (This does not replace regularly monitoring air pressure with a tire gauge.)

When a tire is running seriously low, it'll pull the car to one side and acceleration will become difficult. If you find yourself fighting the steering wheel to keep the car on the road and/or are unable to accelerate as usual, pull over and check your tires. If one is significantly low, do not drive on it, or at least don't drive very far. This is an unsafe tire. You may still even be able to repair the tire rather than have to replace it. Put your spare on or call for help.

If you fail to stop when your air pressure is too low, you may see smoke coming from your vehicle. Heated up like this, a tire low on air can produce *a lot of smoke*. You may not realize the smoke is coming from a tire; you may even think your engine is on fire. At this point it's too late to salvage the tire; it's already destroyed. (Amazingly, some people keep driving even with their car billowing smoke.) If it hasn't already, the tire will soon blow. Once it blows, if you continue driving (yes, some people do), you now risk destroying and having to replace the rim as well. This expensive calamity is 100% preventable.

Some vehicles have built-in Tire Pressure

Monitoring Systems (TPMS) that monitor the air pressure for you, alerting you when your tires are under- or over-inflated. TPMS may be set too low so that by the time they warn you, your tires may have already reached an inflation level that is too low, and too late to prevent irreparable damage.

With or without a TPMS, it's up to you to keep an eye on things. Visual checks of your tires can help prevent problems, but can also be misleading. A tire can lose up to 50% of its pressure and not appear to be flat. To maintain proper inflation, check the pressure regularly using a tire gauge. (Check tire air pressure while the tire is cold.)

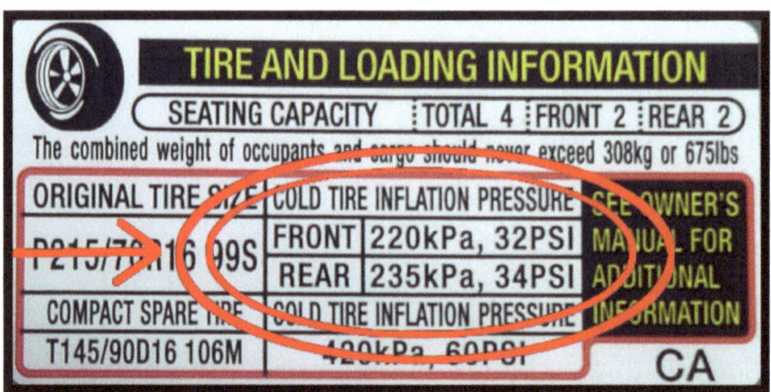

Refer to your owner's manual or the tire inflation decal chart (located on your car's door jam, door post, fuel door, or glove box) for the auto manufacturer's recommended psi (pounds per square inch). Take this recommendation very seriously - lives depend on it.

If you don't know how much air to put in, 32-34 psi

is a safe range for most tires, and can be used until you are able to confirm the psi that is recommended for your tires.

The maximum psi for a tire is molded (in tiny print) directly on the sidewall of every tire. **Do not inflate the tire beyond this number.**

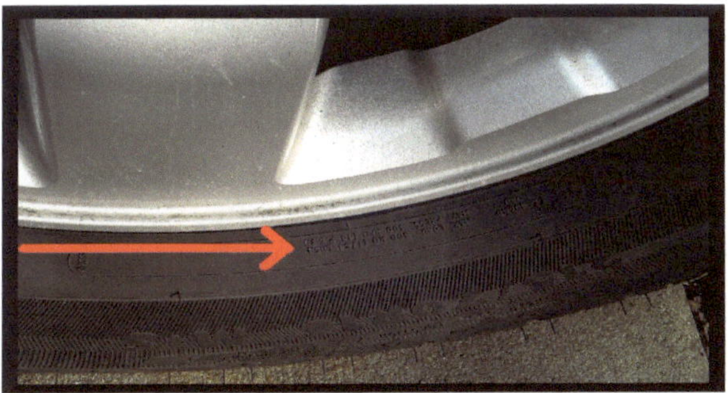

We are talking about proper inflation of five tires, not four. (Read more under "The Spare.") The exception to this is "run flat" tires which are designed to resist deflating when punctured, enabling the tire to be driven at reduced speeds for limited distances. If you are unsure whether or not you have "run-flat" tires, you probably don't.

Changes in weather affect your tires. For every 10º F (18º C) change in the outdoor temperature, the pressure in your tires changes by about 1-2 psi. Be sure to monitor accordingly.

Properly maintained, most tires today will go 50,000 miles or more.

● The Spare

We have a tendency to forget about our spare tires. What? You don't *have* a spare? Correct that situation immediately!

It's a dang good idea to know how to change a flat yourself. Car manufacturers strive to make the tire-changing process easy enough that virtually anyone can do it.

Most cars come equipped with a jack, lug wrench, and spare tire. Be sure you know where to locate these items and that your spare tire is in good shape. If it's not, get it fixed. Yeah, it's a hassle, but imagine yourself going to replace a flat tire and discovering your spare is flat. You're going to replace a flat with a flat? It only takes minute. Just do it.

The lug wrenches that come standard with vehicles are probably not going to be the tool you actually want to use should you need to change a flat. You'll want something more substantial. Heavy-duty universal 4-way lug wrench are not very expensive. It's well worth the money to have one on hand should you need it. And unlike the lug wrench that comes with your auto, the universal 4-way wrench fits lug nuts on most vehicles, not just yours, better equipping you to assist a stranded fellow-driver.

Whenever tires are removed, the lug nuts need to

be put back on in a star pattern, evenly, in the right order, and using the right tightness. If they are not put back on properly, you'll end up with premature rotor wear and it'll be taking more money out of your wallet... and sooner than you'd like.

● Nitrogen

The latest innovation in tire air is nitrogen. Nitrogen replaces thinner oxygen molecules with fatter nitrogen molecules. A tire filled with nitrogen retains optimal air pressure longer, runs cooler, wears more uniformly, and gets better gas mileage. Even with nitrogen, still monitor your tire air pressure on a regular basis.

● Rotation

As tires wear, they develop a wear pattern. Rotating tires from one position to another prolongs the life of the wearing-down tire. The type of tire, the tire's position on the car, and the drive mechanism of your vehicle all influence the wear pattern. See your tire professional to determine which position each tire should be rotated from and to.

Rule of thumb: Rotate your tires every 5,000 - 8,000 miles.

● Tire Seasons

Driving in snow, sleet, or ice can be difficult, and at

times downright dangerous. The right tires on your vehicle can provide *huge* handling and safety advantages when trekking through snowy or wet conditions.

It's not a bad idea to swap out all four summer tires for four beefier snow tires in the winter. Then your summer driving miles are not wearing out the grip of your tires that will be safer for your winter driving miles.

Owning two sets of tires can be a bit of an expense up front, but you'll only be putting half the miles on each set every year, so you can run each set twice as long. With two sets of tires, you'll also get the bonus of automatic tire rotations twice a year.

The other option is all-season tires that you drive year-round. The advantages of all-season tires are that you don't have to change the tires before and after winter, and you don't have to keep two sets of tires and rims. The disadvantage is you don't get all the great features of a specialized seasonal tire.

Do not run summer tires in winter conditions.

● Tread

In a nutshell, the job of the tread on your tires is to move water out of the way on wet roads. As tread-depth wears down, your tire's ability to disperse water diminishes. Performance and safety while driving in rain and snow require more tread than in dry conditions.

Driving on snowy roads, tires should have at least 6/32" of remaining tread. With less tread than that, necessary traction and stability become compromised.

Driving in rain or on wet roads, tires will ideally have at least 4/32" of remaining tread.

The drop-dead bottom line is 2/32" of tread depth. At 2/32", traction is significantly compromised, resistance to hydroplaning is virtually eliminated, and you're just plain asking for serious trouble. Replace the tire.

A bald tire is a disaster waiting to happen. If your tread is too low, *replace the tire*. New tires seem expensive, but they're abso-dang-lutely inexpensive in every way compared to a nasty accident.

Hydroplaning

Hydroplaning literally means "floating on top of water." Eventually tire tread wears to a point where even mild, misty rain can cause hydroplaning. When tires hydroplane, they lose contact with the road, leaving your car out of control. Hitting the brakes, stepping on the accelerator, or trying to steer your way out of it is useless. When your tires don't have contact with the surface of the road, they cannot respond to your driving commands.

You simply have no control over the vehicle.

Braking when hydroplaning is the *worst* thing you can do. Stopping the tires makes them unable to remove the water at all and will put the car into a skid. Keeping off the brake and off the accelerator is your best bet. This allows the vehicle to keep moving through the water and get to a spot where the tires can regain traction. Hydroplaning doesn't happen just because you have worn tires. New tires can hydroplane. It's the volume of water relative to the depth of the tread that causes hydroplaning. If there's too much water for the tread depth, any tire can lose contact with the road surface and hydroplane.

● Siping

John Sipe was a boater who cut grooves into the soles of his shoes to get more traction on boat decks. This practice evolved into the cutting of small grooves in the tread blocks on tires and is known as "siping." The cuts allow the tread blocks to spread apart, which forces water out of the tread, producing better traction, better tire flexibility, and reducing wear on your tire. Siping increases tire life and results in a smoother ride.

● Stranded

Especially before starting out on a road trip, check inflation and take a look at your tires. Look for any unevenly worn spots or skimpy tread. If the tires are iffy, invest in new ones. You'll need them eventually anyway, and it's better to start out on a trip with new tires than have a blowout in the middle of nowhere.

A flat tire caused by picking up a nail or other sharp object may be able to eek out a few miles by using an emergency puncture sealant spray. However, these sprays should be used (following the manufacturer's directions) only if necessary. The repair shop may charge you extra to remove the substance from your tire, and if you use the spray in a tire from a vehicle with a Tire Pressure Monitoring System, plan on replacing the sensor, too. They can be spendy.

HOW TO CHECK TIRE AIR PRESSURE

Do not exceed the maximum pressure rating (psi) noted on the sidewall of the tire.

You can use a traditional or digital tire gauge. The traditional tire gauge has one end that fits on the tire valve, and the other end that has a pressure measuring stick protruding.

1) Check air pressure when the tire is **cold**. This is important.

2) Remove the cap from the valve stem.

3) If using a traditional gauge, make sure the measurement stick is pressed as far into the tire gauge as it goes.

4) Quickly and firmly place the end with the round opening on the valve stem, creating a tight seal.

5) The measurement stick of the traditional gauge will pop out the other end. The highest number you see on the stick is the amount of pressure in your tire. Or…

6) The number shown on the display of a digital gauge will be the amount of pressure in your tire. Neither gauge will read correctly if you do not get a quick seal on the valve.

7) For accuracy, repeat until you get the same reading twice.

8) If your air pressure is low, add air.

9) Be sure to securely replace valve caps.

<u>HOW TO MEASURE TREAD DEPTH:</u>

No special tools are needed to assess tread depth. A simple penny can be used.

Place a penny (minted prior to 2010) into a groove in the tire. If you *cannot* see the hair on the top of Lincoln's head, you have more than 2/32" of tread depth remaining. The tire is still ok.

If you *can* see the hair on the top of Lincoln's head, the tire needs to go. The tire in this photo is almost to that drop-dead bottom-line point. There are "wear bars" molded into tires to alert you when you have reached that drop-dead replace the tire point. If you're one to run the tires to the very end, learn to read the wear bars.

Tires wear unevenly, so check the tread depth in each groove across the depth of the tire, then check the remainder of the tire by placing the measuring coin into four or five locations around the circumference of the tire.

Many safety-conscious motorists will not let their tires wear down anywhere near the seriously low 2/32" level. Many will replace their tires at or above the 4/32" measurement.

<u>HOW TO CHANGE A FLAT TIRE</u>

1) If you're on the road, **find a safe spot to pull over.** If you're on the freeway,

getting off is the safest, even if you have to drive on a blown tire. Otherwise, pull as far onto the shoulder as possible. Even off to the side, freeways are dangerous places to stop. Don't park on a curve, under or on a bridge, or where approaching cars can't see you. Choose as flat a spot as possible. Jacking up your car on a hill can be disastrous. Leave manual transmissions in gear. Set your parking brake.

2) If you're on the freeway, getting off is the safest, even if you have to drive on a blown tire.

3) **Turn on the hazard lights.**

4) **Get the jack, lug wrench, and spare tire from the trunk** and bring them over to the tire that is flat.

5) **Loosen the lug nuts.** If you have hubcaps, you'll have to remove them. Do not *remove* the lug nuts yet, just loosen them by turning the wrench left (counter-clockwise). If the lug nuts are too tight, place the wrench on the nut and step on the wrench with your full weight.

6) **Raise the vehicle off the ground with the jack.** Vehicles have different

recommended secure places underneath to put the jack to prevent damaging the vehicle; consult your owner's manual for your vehicle's specified location. With the jack securely in the correct spot, jack the car up until the tire is about six inches off the ground.

7) **Raise the vehicle off the ground with the jack.** Vehicles have recommended secure places underneath to put the jack to prevent damaging the vehicle; consult your owner's manual for your vehicle's specified location. With the jack securely in the correct spot, jack the car up until the tire is about 6" off the ground.

8) **Remove the lug nuts.** Keep the lug nuts together in a pile so they don't get dirty or lost. (Putting dirty lug nuts back on can create more problems down the road.) Pull the tire straight off to remove it from the wheelbase. If you have trouble getting the tire off, don't try jiggling it too much. Jiggling can knock the car off the jack. If the tire is stuck in place, driving on it with the lug nuts loosened might help. To do this, loosen the lug nuts, then drive the car a short distance; a couple of feet may be all it takes.

9) **Put the spare on the car.** Line up the lug nut posts with the holes in the spare, and push the spare onto the wheelbase as far as it can go.

10) **Put the lug nuts back on.** Don't put them on tight yet. Snug them enough for the spare to stay on the car for now.

11) **Lower the car back to the ground.** Use the jack to bring the car back down, then remove the jack from under the car.

12) Whenever tires are removed, the **lug nuts need to be put back on in a star pattern**, evenly, in the right order, and using the right tightness. If they are not put back on properly, you'll end up with premature rotor wear.

13) **Tighten the lug nuts.** Don't tighten them in consecutive order, and don't tighten them all the way. Follow this pattern: tighten one lug nut about 50%, then tighten a nut situated opposite that one, again tightening it about 50% of the way. Gradually tighten all the lug nuts about 50%, alternating each time to a nut situated relatively-opposite the one you just tightened. Then, following the same pattern, tighten each lug nut all the way. Lighter-weight motorists, go ahead and

tighten them as tight as you can get them. Heavier-weights, get them tight, but don't break them.

CHAPTER 5

BRAKES

The whole idea behind cars is to get us moving and where we want to go. But just as what goes up must come down, going doesn't happen without the requisite accompanying stopping. This is where we get into another critical automotive component: brakes. Again, brake problems can become more than a financial deficit, their performance (or lack thereof) can be life altering. Don't ignore the signs.

For starters, **riding your brake** wears your pads, warps your rotors, and is harder on the transmission too. Unless you are in the act of slowing or stopping your vehicle, get your foot off the brake.

A lot of city driving and **frequent stops** and starts wears the brakes faster. If this is the type of driving you do, get a brake inspection once a year.

And it should go without saying, but I'll say it anyway. If your **brake warning light** comes on, well of course... get in to see your car care professional.

Like all car parts, brakes are going to wear out over time. If you sense something is not right, get it checked out. Sooner rather than later. It's not worth putting anybody at unnecessary risk. And like many of car maintenance matters, the longer you put it off, the more likely you'll have bigger repair bills.

Pay attention. Sounds, smells and sensations can be alerting you to brake problems.

● Sounds

If you hear squealing, squeaking, grinding, screeching or other sharp noises, think brakes. If you start hearing a high-pitched noise and it stops when you apply the brakes, there's a good chance your brake pads have an issue. Your pads are probably worn out and need to be replaced. Ignore it and the damage will worsen and rotors will end up needing replacement too. This is an expensive and can easily be avoided.

If the sound you are hearing is a grinding, a number of different things could be causing it. Could be something minor like dust, or could be much more than that. If you hear (or feel) grinding in your brakes, get in to see your car care professional promptly.

● Sensations

If what you're feeling is a shaking in the steering wheel, or a vibration or pulsation when you apply the brakes, same thing goes. Get in to see your car care professional. Promptly.

Noticing a **spongy brake pedal**? Get it looked at by your car care professional.

Noticing a **decrease in the resistance in the brake peda**l... a soft brake pedal or the pedal is sinking all the way to the floor when depressed? Get it looked at by your car care professional IMMEDIATELY.

- **Smells**

A burning or chemical odor after hard braking on steep roads is a sign of overheated brakes or clutch. Safely pull over immediately, make sure your parking brake is fully released and let the brakes cool off. If you don't let them cool off, it can cause brake failure.

BRAKE FLUID

If your brake fluid light comes on, you have a serious situation. Do not add brake fluid and think you've solved the problem. If your brake fluid is low, something is crucially wrong. Adding fluid will only mask a dangerous problem. **If your brake fluid light comes on, get your brakes checked immediately!**

CHAPTER 5

BATTERY

Properly maintained, batteries last about five years. An inexpensive battery may last a year or two less; a higher-quality battery may last a year or two more. Plan to replace yours about that often. If your battery is not getting enough charge to easily start your car, have it checked. Most car batteries come with warranties.

If your battery is dead, you don't necessarily have to purchase a new one. A battery can often be brought back to life by jumpstarting it using jumper cables (you have cables, right?) or by connecting the battery to a battery charger. If you frequently experience a dead battery, have a mechanic check the battery, the charging system, and draws on the battery.

JUMPER CABLES

Certain vehicles should not be jump-started (typically higher-end vehicles). Jumping-starting may damage the electrical systems. For these, it's recommended to disconnect the battery and charge it. If you are unsure if it's safe to jump your battery, refer to your owner's manual.

Jumper cables are used to start a vehicle with a dead battery. Own jumper cables, carry them in your vehicle, and know how to use them.

To jump start your car, along with jumper cables, you'll need the assistance of another vehicle with a fully charged battery. There's no point in beginning the jumpstarting procedure if you don't have another car available to jump the dead battery from.

Jump-starting needs to be done correctly, connecting the cables in the proper order and disconnecting the cables in the proper order!

First, determine if you actually need to jump your battery. If you turn the key in the ignition and your vehicle makes a click but won't start, you probably need to jump start it. If the vehicle makes a starting noise and devices such as your lights and radio work, then the battery is not your problem. In this case, jumper cables probably won't help.

HOW TO USE JUMPER CABLES

NOTE: Certain vehicles should not be jump-started (typically higher-end vehicles). Jumping-starting may damage the electrical components.

The recommendation for these autos is to disconnect the battery and charge it. If you are unsure if it's safe to jump-start your battery, refer to your owner's manual.

Determine if you actually need to jump your battery. If you turn the key in the ignition and your vehicle makes a click but won't start, you need to jump start it. If the vehicle makes a starting noise and devices such as your lights and radio work, then the battery is not your problem. In this case, jumper cables won't help.

Use caution. Batteries contain acid, and the hydrogen and oxygen gasses involved can cause a violent explosion. ***It's important to do this properly.*** Wearing safety goggles is recommended.

1) Park a vehicle with a fully charged battery next to the vehicle with the dead battery. (Leave this engine running.) The two batteries must be close enough so the jumper cables can reach both of them.

2) Raise both hoods.

3) Keep the ends (the metal clips) of the jumper cables separated from each other. Do not let them touch each other during the jumping process.

4) Attach one of the red clips of the jumper cable to the metal part of the positive terminal of the dead battery. (A "+" sign indicates the positive terminal. The positive terminal may be slightly larger than the negative terminal.) You may need to remove a plastic cover on the terminal.

5) Attach the other red clip in the same manner to the metal part of the positive terminal of the fully charged battery in the other car.

6) Attach the black clip (the one right next to the red one you just attached in Step 6) to the metal part of the negative terminal of the fully charged battery of the assisting car (indicated by a "-" sign on the battery).

7) Making sure you are not touching any metal parts, clamp the remaining black clip to any piece of heavy metal within the engine of the car with the dead battery. Do not clamp it to lines, hoses, or non-heavy-metal parts. (Don't panic if your cable sparks a bit when

you make contact.)

8) Try starting the vehicle with the dead battery. It should start right up. If it doesn't, check to be sure the jumper cable connections are secure and making good contact.

9) If the engine starts, do not turn the engine off until after you drive the vehicle for a while. The now-revived battery needs to build up a charge, which it can do only with the engine running.

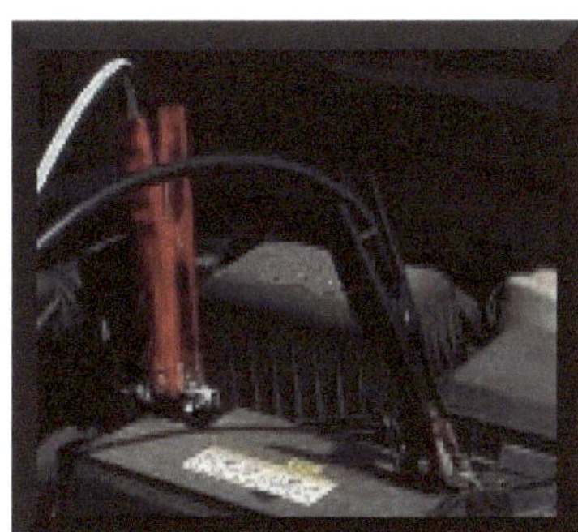

10) If the engine does not start, seek advice from your mechanic or other automotive professional.

DISCONNECT THE JUMPER CABLES IN THE REVERSE ORDER:

1. Remove the black clip from the dead battery.

2. Remove the black clip from the charged battery.

3. Remove the red clip on the charged battery.

4. Remove the red clip from the dead battery.

CHAPTER 6

TRANSMISSION

The majority of **damage to transmissions is caused by heat**. Other damaging factors can be old transmission fluid, excessive braking, over-accelerating in hot weather, and towing trailers.

Experts recommend that with severe use of your car (using your car in heavy city traffic and at temperatures over 90 F for more than 50% of your driving time) you should have the transmission filter and fluid changed every 15,000 miles. If your car use is less severe, or in cooler weather, the recommended maintenance is usually between 25,000 and 60,000 miles. Your car manual or car care professional can tell you the optimum number for your vehicle. If you do towing or other unusual driving, again, talk to your car care professional for their recommendation.

Regular transmission fluid and filter maintenance helps **prevent fluid oxidization**, which can end up hardening rubber seals and gaskets, which will then start leaking. Preventative maintenance with your transmission can save you a lot of money.

Transmission fluid should be bright red in color, which you can check by wiping a small amount on a cotton ball or a piece of white paper, and should smell slightly sweet. While you can usually check the transmission fluid yourself, the draining and changing of it should be handled by a professional, especially with an automatic transmission.

Don't overfill your transmission fluid. Doing so can cause the fluid to foam, lead to erratic shifting, loss of internal lubrication, and potential transmission damage.

Low transmission fluid leads to problems. **Fill low transmission fluid** as quickly as possible and avoid driving your vehicle when fluid is below the recommended level.

Every time you shift from drive to reverse or reverse to drive, stop the vehicle completely before shifting to the other gear. Complete stops between shifting to and from these gears prevents unnecessary strain on your transmission.

CHAPTER 7

FUSES

The way your car protects itself from short-circuits and power overloads is to blow fuses. This clever mechanism prevents serious equipment damage or even fire. Fuses are inexpensive and easy to replace.

Often a fuse will blow due to a momentary overload. The horn, radio, air conditioner, or interior light, for example, may stop working. Replacing the bad fuse should fix the problem. Be sure to replace a fuse with a fuse of the right amperage.

If a fuse blows repeatedly, it indicates an electrical problem that will require a trip to your mechanic.

HOW TO CHANGE A FUSE

Your owner's manual will show you where your vehicle's fuse panel is located.

1) Remove the fuse panel cover. You'll see several color-coded fuses plugged in. These colors, along with the numbers stamped on the bottoms or sides of the fuses, indicate different amperage ratings. Turn over the fuse panel cover to see the fuse diagram showing which fuse works with which electrical component.

2) You have to find the faulty one. It will have a broken or melted filament (the thin strip of metal inside) or will be black inside. Some vehicles come with special pullers to remove fuses, or you can use needle-nose pliers or your fingers. ***Carefully*** remove and replace the fuses one at a time until you find the culprit. If none of the fuses look blown, seek advice from your mechanic or other automotive professional.

3) Unless you know you have correct amperage fuses in to begin with, it's not a bad idea to double-check the slot in the fuse panel to make sure the blown fuse you remove from the slot is actually the amperage that should be in that slot.

4) Use the fuse panel diagram and the color-coded fuses to determine the correct amperage. Replace the blown fuse with a new fuse of the correct amperage. If you use the wrong amperage, you could cause more damage than just a blown fuse. Place the new fuse in the

correct slot and push down gently but firmly to ensure it's completely installed. Replace the fuse panel cover.

5) Start the vehicle to see if the circuit is now working properly. If it is, you probably just had a temporary overload that caused the fuse to blow. If the circuit doesn't work, or it works only briefly before it needs to be replaced again, the problem is beyond a blown fuse. Check it out with your car care specialist.

   If you don't have a new fuse available, as long as the amperage is the right, you can temporarily take the fuse from another less-used fuse socket, like the cigarette lighter, radio, or rear window heater, and use it for your blown fuse.

CHAPTER 8

LIGHTS

Burned out light bulbs jeopardize safety. If you're driving in front of someone and you plan to make a turn, the guy behind you only knows to prepare for your turn if he sees your turn-signal light flashing. If the lamp's not working, he can't see it. I'm sure I don't need to spell out for you that you would now be predisposed to getting rear-ended. Then you and he both may have to commence with filling out a police report, calling insurance companies, getting repair estimates, having bodywork done. Sheesh.

Routinely check your bulbs, replacing any that are burned out. It's quick and easy to do. A parking space in front of a glass storefront is perfect for this. While parked in front of the glass, turn on your various lights, and observe the reflection bouncing off the glass to confirm each light's performance. Back in to assess the lights in the rear of the car. Using a garage door or other wall-type surface works for this also. Or just sit in your car and have a comrade look on, giving you a thumbs up for each light that works.

Be sure to check them all:

- Headlights - high beams and low beams
- Right and left turn signals - front and back
- Tail lights and brake lights
- Back-up lights
- Hazard lights - front and back

If one bulb is out, it's probably a burned out bulb. If multiple lights are out, check fuses instead.

Burned out bulbs can also catch you a fine. Do you really want to throw your money into that pit? It's worth a minute of your time once in a while to check bulbs.

CHAPTER 9

FLUIDS

Keep an eye on fluids in their reservoirs, as well as any fluids leaking underneath your vehicle. Fluids seen leaking under a vehicle could be power steering, brake, or transmission fluid, oil, or water from the air-conditioner. Dripping or leaking liquid other than water from your air conditioner should be checked out. (The AC will not drip water under the car if have not been running the AC.)

If you suspect something is dripping, put a piece of cardboard under your vehicle while it's parked, then later check the cardboard to see if any fluids have dripped on it.

The most important fluids to monitor regularly include:

- Windshield washer (Very important to have in certain conditions.)
- Engine oil (You already know this, right?)
- Antifreeze/coolant (Never remove the

radiator cap while the engine is hot.)
- Brake (Check with engine off or running.)
- Power-steering (Check with engine off.)
- Transmission (Check with engine running.)

Engine fluids usually have containers with fill-level lines. Make sure the fluids are above the minimum line and below the maximum line.

CHAPTER 10

SOME INCIDENTALS

ALIGNMENT

Misalignment of wheels can cause rapid wearing of your tires. Have your alignment checked when you feel "pulling" or have some other indication the handling is not right. Hitting potholes, objects lying in the road, curbs, etc., can throw your wheels out of alignment.

WINDSHIELD WIPERS

Winter conditions are hard on wipers. So are particularly sunny conditions. Depending on where you live, the rubber portion of the wiper generally lasts six months to a year. You can replace just the rubber portion or you can change the whole arm and blade. Your local auto parts store can help you be sure you get the correct replacement wipers.

SALT

Salt speeds up the corrosion of vehicles and is a particular problem for auto-owners who live near a salty ocean or in cold climates where salt is used to melt ice on the roads. To help prevent or slow down corrosion:

- Wash your car regularly, especially during the winter where road salt is used.

- Do an underbody wash from time-to-time, especially in the spring where road salt is used. (Dirt stuck to the underbody holds salt and speeds chassis corrosion.)

- It's not always bad news. A client brings her car in to Pudge for service. She's having a **cornering issue**. Every time she turns a corner, the car produces a loud clunk. Doesn't matter if it's righthand turn or a lefthand turn. Every turn clunks. And she is very concerned about the 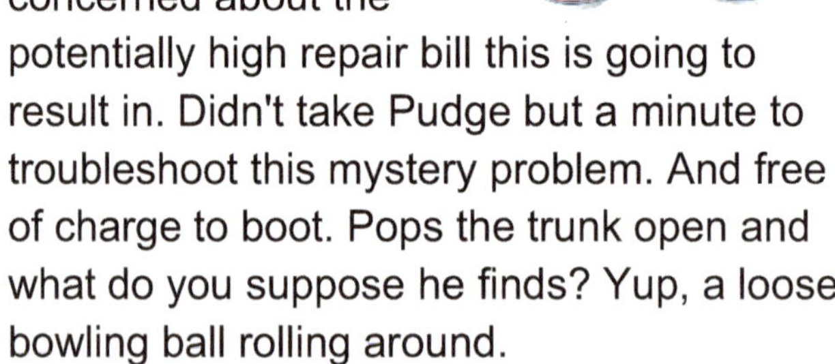 potentially high repair bill this is going to result in. Didn't take Pudge but a minute to troubleshoot this mystery problem. And free of charge to boot. Pops the trunk open and what do you suppose he finds? Yup, a loose bowling ball rolling around.

- Don't use **cruise control in wet or snowy conditions**. A wet surface can easily break the contact between your tires and the road surface. This loss of contact causes a loss of control. (Read more under "Hydroplaning.") When hydroplaning, hitting the brakes is the worst thing you can do. If the cruise control is on when your tires lose contact with the road, the cruise control will keep your vehicle accelerating, sending you even further out of control. If you lose traction on the road, it's important to deactivate the cruise control if you have it on.

- If you find yourself heading into an accident, shift your attention off the problem and onto the solution. **Don't look at what you're trying to avoid**. Instead, **focus your eyes on where you want your vehicle to go** to avoid the potential impact. Is there a lane open on either side of you? Is there shoulder space on the road, or is there a guard rail or median you would hit? Where you put your attention is the path your vehicle is more likely to follow.

- Don't be a **freeway vigilante**. I used to drive 55 mph in the fast lane; I was going to teach those speedsters to drive the speed limit! One of the most valuable lessons I've learned was that I wasn't teaching anybody anything, nor was I making traffic any safer. All I was doing was slowing down traffic and making fellow-motorists mad. Sage advice told me to just get over and let them pass. Live and let live.

- **Use Your Blinkers**. It's how other drivers know what you intend to do, and it's how you know what other drivers intend to do. That tiny blinking light can prevent a multitude of fender benders, scrapes, and full blown accidents. C'mon everybody, use them.

- It isn't something that happens often, but if you ever find yourself in a **runaway car**, put the car in neutral. Do NOT turn the engine off. Turning the engine off also turns off your power steering and brakes, which you'll need. Slipping the transmission into neutral is the safest reaction.

- The **"move over" law** requires drivers to move over by one lane when approaching stationary emergency vehicles with sirens or lights activated. If you can't move over, you must slow down 20 mph (32kmh) below the posted speed limit. On roads with only one lane going each direction, you must move out of the way as much as possible. Drivers can be charged with, for example, 15 years in prison and/or a $7,500 fine for causing injury or death to emergency personnel.

- For **emergency vehicles** approaching from

either direction (from behind or coming at you), motorists must pull over to the right side of the road. On roads with multiple same-way lanes, pull to either side. If a fence or other divider separates you from the lane the emergency vehicle is in, you don't need to pull over.

- The **cost of owning a vehicle** continually lessens the longer you keep the car. Keeping a vehicle for a longer period of time can save you bucks.

- **Keeping the same car** after it's paid off can save you some serious money. With no car payments, and the price of tabs and insurance steadily decreasing, long-term ownership can put ka-ching back in your pocket.

- Keep an eye out for and repair or replace leaking, brittle, cracked, rusted, loose or worn **belts, tubes, or wires** under your hood.

- To clean **corrosion buildup** off your battery terminals, pour a mixture of baking soda and warm water over the corrosion. Use as much soda as you need. Rinse with water. You can use Coca-Cola to clean corrosion too. I favor baking soda. (Baking soda is great in the house too. But that's a topic from our household book in the *Now You Know* series.)

- Repairing **paint chips** can keep corrosion from infecting at a weak spot. You can use "touch-up" paint. To match the color accurately, you'll want to do a bit of research to make sure you match the paint code number for your vehicle.

- **Deep cracks in tires** can cause blowouts. If you have cracks in your tires, ask your tire technician if they are deep enough to be of concern.

- If you see a car headed towards you from the front or rear that you think is going to hit you, **slip your car into neutral** to allow your vehicle to move more freely upon impact, helping to decrease impact intensity.

- **Driving requires your attention.** Texting or accessing the internet on a wireless device while driving is a bad idea and a bad habit. Don't do it.

- **Use your emergency brake** when parking on an incline. This reduces stress on the parking pin and linkage.

- Sitting in your car with the hood raised is a **distress signal**. Utilize this practice if you need help. If you don't need help, don't sit this way.

- **Waxing** your car just twice a year can greatly help guard against scratches and keep your car looking like new.

- Make sure your **air filter** is inspected at each oil change.

- Allow your engine to **warm up on cold winter starts.** Warming up the engine/transmission for about 30 seconds to a minute before driving is best practice.

- This guidebook will help you with the basics, but there's nothing like real-life experience. Don't hesitate to **ask your mechanic or tire professional** to help you identify parts, understand functions, or share their knowledge with you.

- If it's rainy enough to turn your wipers on, turn on your **headlights** too.

- Keep the **owner's manual** in the vehicle.

You may want to keep a few basics in your auto. They might never get used, they might turn out to be little comforts in a casually adverse situation, or they might save a life. Weird and unexpected stuff happens on this planet. A little preparedness can go a long way.

Inside the car… easily accessible:

- Towel (you're caught in a downpour, a liquid spills, you know the stuff)

- Paper napkins in glove box
- Tire gauge
- Ladies: tampons, pads, travel-size deodorant (you just never know)

In the trunk:

- Hat, gloves, sweatshirt, jacket, rain jacket
- Puncture sealant spray
- Some lighter-weight rope or twine
- Blanket (nice for that impromptu picnic or concert in the park, too)

If you're the, um, *more negligent* type who doesn't stay on top of routine auto maintenance and are more likely to run into problems on the road, you might consider keeping in you car:

- Motor oil
- Washer fluid
- Engine coolant

That about covers it. None of this is difficult. Anyone who owns a car should be able to adopt the practice of these simple car care steps. Awareness and application, that's all it takes.

One final note, please share this information. The more educated motorists there are on our roadways, properly maintaining their vehicles and driving conscientiously, defensively and wisely, the better life will be for us all. It's up to us as drivers to cultivate harmony and safety on our roadways. If every driver makes even a marginal effort to make traffic flow more smoothly and courteously when a proverbial "bump in the road" comes along while motoring, our world would be a better place indeed.

Oh, and in case you missed the previous occurrences of this one...
Driving requires your attention. Texting or accessing the internet on a wireless device while driving is a bad idea and a bad habit. Don't do it. Don't do it. **Don't do it.**

Have any suggestions you'd like to see added to a future book revision? Let me know at lauren1056@gmail.com.

It is my honor to share this experience with you.

If this guide book has helped any motorist along their way, I am thankful for having been able to assist.

May this guidebook serve you and your loved ones well for years to come, hopefully helping you to stretch your automotive dollars and to know nothing but happy and safe travels!

DISCLAIMER

Proper service and repair procedures are vital to the safe, reliable operation of all motor vehicles. Standard safety procedures and precautions (including use of safety goggles and proper tools and equipment) should be followed at all times to prevent injury or damage to the vehicle.

This material has been prepared with the intent to provide car care information. No warranty, express or implied, is made as to its accuracy or completeness, nor is any liability assumed for loss or damage resulting from reliance on this material. Neither the author nor publisher is liable for damages of any type arising out of the use of this material.

MAINTENANCE LOG

Glove Box Guide Maintenance Log

Vehicle make, model & year:

VIN: _______________________________

License Plate #:_____________________

Service Performed	Mileage	Date

Glove Box Guide Maintenance Log

Vehicle make, model & year:

VIN: ________________________________

License Plate #:________________________

Service Performed	Mileage	Date